Michael Oropollo, Jr.

COVER IMAGE: U.S. Government – Public Domain
BOOK DESIGN – LIBERO MEDIA
AUTHOR PHOTO – D. PISARRA

PUBLISHER:

LIBERO MEDIA
1305 PICO BLVD
SANTA MONICA, CA 90405

Thoughts

PREFACE

I've always had a fascination with human behavior and society. Most of my writings, both in this book and for outside contributions, are observations of people and their behavior as it relates to the broader societal narrative.

When I began writing this piece, the idea was to write a compilation book of totally independent stories. But as the collection grew I began to see a thread that connected them together. They all seemed to build off of each other.

The connecting thread was the human experience, and thew human experience as it relates to our society.

The pieces in this book were written as independent pieces over the course of several months and are all social commentary works. Some of the topics I write about are politics, race, fame, and spirituality. I wrote some deeply serious pieces, and some funny, absurd ones.

The first piece, "The State of Current Affairs", was the very last story I wrote. I wanted to paint a back drop for the stories to take place in, as well as set a starting point for the rest of the book to branch out from.

The rest is 48 additional stories, independent, but connected, creating a single body of work. It is designed to be an introspective look into society, ourselves, and the relationship between the two.

Each time I read through, the meaning changes and the plot shifts. I have read it through the eyes of single protagonist as well as through the eyes of several protagonists.

This book is intended to raise many questions and provide limited answers. Several of the stories are left open ended. They are designed for you to draw your own conclusions and meaning.

Michael Oropollo, Jr.

The State of Current Affairs
I.

Atrophied gangsters
Of the fourth reich,
Flick a line chart
With their decrepit fingers,
Send the markets tumbling
Down the stairs.
Grabbing fistfuls
Of Goldie locks hair
Cackling laughs and coughing
Up their diseased phlegm.
They light up cigars
Of hundred dollar bills.
And throw dinosaurs
Into the coal engine of
The capitalist machine.
The disenfranchised hyenas,
Who can't spend
Their trust fund fast enough,
Dress themselves in costumes
Of Mother Theresa.
Hiding away in a dirty backroom,
In their adorned temple of Mao,
Boiling the world's problems
Down to 3 rules and 8 points.
Hangs a sign on the front door that says,
"No public restroom."
Robotic humans, significantly less intelli-
gent,
Than the AI they replaced,
But who will work for less money
Answer the phone,
And respond
"I have no opinion on that matter.
Or any matters."

Thoughts

The pineal gland dormant and catatonic
An appendage made possible by the current hu-
man evolution.
A mountain, product of millions of years
Of erosion reflects off the water an exact
copy.
The copy ripples and distorts when a child
Throws a stone into it.
The original always remains pure.

Michael Oropollo, Jr.

The Machine

II.

I was born in a factory in northeastern Mis-
souri.
Through the labyrinth of machine,
Swaged and pressed.
Copper and Lead.
Down the conveyor belt,
fondled and inspected.
I am the perfect shape.
The right weight.
Optimal diameter.
I was born and thrown into a cart
with thousands just like me.
From the TV screen to theaters of war.
Down the runway and out of the barrel of a
gun.
To influence the minds of the mindless,
At home and abroad.
I am the perfect shape,
The right weight.
Optimal diameter.

III.

Superior court of America,
Such an inferior system.
Cobwebs of bureaucracy
Tangle up your time,
Precious, precious time.
Chewed and swallowed
By the ogre of justice.
Obsolete humans
With way too important a job,
Gatekeepers of our most scarce commodity,
Time.
One copy of your document?
That'll be a couple hundred dollars,
And a couple hundred hours.
The front of the line I've finally reached.
"Lunch time, please come back tomorrow."
The wheels of justice grind so slow,
It's amazing they don't grind to a stop.
But the scales of justice are made of gold,
The bottom line in justice is never justice,
The bottom line is always the bottom line.

IV.

I grew up on the wrong side a the tracks,
ruff neighbahood ya know but it was arrite.
Came from a good family, white picket fence.
Dad worked his 9-5, Mom stayed home wit the
kids. Every Sunday the whole family had
dinner togetha, aunts, uncles, the little
kids runnin' around and shit, it was nice. Ya
average American family you could say.
The neighbahood was split up, ya had the
Irish neighbahood north of 7th street, the Jews
were in the East, the Puerto Ricans had South
of Morgan Street and the Italians were right
smack in the middle a all that. And everyone
had their little rackets they was all makin'
money ya know.
Every now on then someone would step on
someone else's toes and there'd be all out war,
but it resolved itself cause no one wanted to
fuck up their money ya know.
Even though they were wiseguys they always
treated us kids arrite. They took care a the
neighbahood. Took care a the kids, the people
in it. I remba this one guy coffee, he'd
carry my grandmotha's groceries all the way
home from the store every time. They used to
play cards togetha every Wednesday night down
at the Bellmont club. One day coffee came
by to say goodbye to my grandmotha, she said
"where ya goin', why you sayin goodbye" but he
knew. Couple weeks later they found him in
those fuckin' swamps next to the 1 & 9 highway.
Fucked up...
But anyways, yea, so I never wanted nuttin
to do with that street shit ya know. I had it

good. Private boarding schools, real fuckin nice ones up in New England and shit all fancy. Graduated near the top of my class, went to one a the best colleges money can buy.

I'd come home for the summa's right, had this little job at the local ice cream joint servin' double scoops heh- heh. But anyways, yea, the neighbahood changed man. These big time guys, way bigga than any a the bosses I had eva seen growin' up moved in. They fuckin' cleared the whole neighbahood out. And not just my neighbahood, all the fuckin' neighbahoods coast to coast. Cleaned up all the rackets, all the guys runnin' numba's, pushin' dope, the loan sharks, every-fuckin'-body.

So anyways, they set up their rackets, which were just like legal versions of the old rackets! The neighbahood started gettin' real fuckin' weird man. They was pushin' dope, but more like pharmaceuticals and shit. But to like pregnant women, and kids, and old folks. Real weird shit. If you wanted to own a business, you had to pay. No if ands or buts about it. And they're hit guys had the military connection, would get all the surplus and shit. Would fuckin' shoot ya if they just felt like you was a threat. Didn't matta who the fuck ya were or what ya did or didn't do.

But yea anyways, these was the guys I wanted to roll with. The big time. Joined their outfit after I got out a my MBA program. Now I got my own crew. I'm a made man. Fuckin' untouchable. I give the people just enough rope to hang themselves and then we swoop in on all the fuckin profits. AND! We got everyone in our pockets. The cops, the

judges, hell, we probably got the fuckin'
president himself on the fuckin' payroll! I
could tank the fuckin' economy and they
wouldn't even be able to write me a goddamn
ticket for it Heh-heh

Well, anyways kid, my 2 o'clock is here, it
was great talkin' to ya, tell your motha I said
hello. Bye now.

Hello Mr. Barrett, nice to see you again.
The markets are doing wonderful, this is the
best time to borrow. Interest rates are low
and don't worry about your credit my lenders
are able to finance you. By the way it's a
pleasure to be able to assist you and your
lovely wife in the purchase of your first
home. You are truly living the American
Dre...

Thoughts

V.

chain link fence
separates the schoolyard from the ghetto.
chain link fence
the division of what's mine and what's yours.
chain link fence
freedom from the prison yard.
Sometimes
You start from one side and end up on the other.
Sometimes
its all that separates you from where you want
to be.
Sometimes
You aren't even sure which side you're on.

VI.

Such great comedy exists,
among our human race.
The greatest of which,
May be the infinite scale
Of black and white.
Humans are cast onto the scale,
No sooner as they come into the world.
Completely unaware of their own place on it,
or the quality they possess
which warrants their placement.
But the machine spits them out
onto the scale.
spitting and placing,
laughing away
cackling a metallic laugh.
That cracks like a whip
whose echo breaks bones.
It's questionable how long the scale has existed,
But it's used in every major decision
regarding the machine.
A virus that found its way so deep
into the operating system,
later versions
made it standard.
No one can tell us
Where the black begins
And the white ends, or
Vice versa.
A laughable error.
That'll tear your heart
Out of your chest
Leave it in a bloody mess,
For someone you love to find.

Thoughts

Break you over
And over and over,
crush the soul out of you,
completely shatter any will
You have to keep living.
A tragic comedy.
A simple broken scale.

Cuba

VII.

Che Guevara came back from the dead,
Rose from under a palm tree in my yard.
I called out
"Che, What was it like"
He said
"O son, death was easy but life was hard"
So I bought him a one way ticket to Cuba,
So he could smoke a cigar with his buddy Fidel,
 "only if you promise to be good this time"
he said
"This time, I wish to raise no hell"
Before he left, he wanted to take a walk
Through Santa Monica, he said he never been,
And as we strolled the promenade
A deep melancholy replaced his grin.
So I looked up with a sense of alert
And saw pretty people of privilege
Wearing his face on their shirt.
"Son, lets get homeward bound"
He crawled back into the hole,
And told me to bury him again,
This time flipped upside down.

VIII.

The 90 minute flight from Miami to cuba
Is as long it takes to get to my aunts house
for Christmas dinner.
As you step off the plane in a small airport,
It's like many other Caribbean island airports,
nothing strikes you different.
Then you step into the streets.
The 90 minutes was more than just a flight,
It was a time portal to the past, to an alien
world.
A flashback to the 1950's,
The old cars, the architecture,
Just how it was left in 1957.
Houses people had lived in,
Made memories in,
Raised families in,
Confiscated and owned by the state,
used however they see fit.
Many times pictures of the family dog,
Still hanging on the wall.
Underneath all of this is a deep air of ten-
sion.
Everyone tells you how happy they are,
How blessed their lives are.
But their worn faces and tired demeanor speak
different words.
The neurotic edginess is palpable.
An air of tension, one that I cannot fully un-
derstand and comprehend
Based on my experiences
Is always present.
A bartender will serve you a cuba libre, just
like in Miami.

Michael Oropollo, Jr.

Except with an overwhelming aura of serious-
ness.
Barroom small talk and bartender commentary
isn't available for me here.
But,
Wearing a Yankees shirt will strike up a glee-
ful conversation of baseball.
Walk on the Malecon at night
And listen to one of the many street bands
playing music
Just for the pure joy of it.
And you can dance with a beautiful girl from
Havana
A law student at the state university, a teach-
er, a nurse
She'll gladly teach you a tango, and laugh with
you.
And share a human connection that bridges
Both culture and politics.

IX.

Obama lifted the embargo today,
rum and cigars,
Another crack in the levee
That will soon be broken.
Rich gringos everywhere rejoiced.
Their life in turmoil,
Over whether their wife
Will find out about their mistress.
Bonuses not as healthy as last years.
But thank god at least they will be able
To have a glass of Havana Club,
With their Cohiba.
Eager developers
Eagerly await.
And real estate moguls
with hawkish eyes
circle over Havana.
Piranhas.
Waiting for the first
Drop of blood to touch the water,
A violent feeding frenzy will surely ensue.
Reckless abandon, gotta get mine.
Harlem, New York City
Venice, California
Havana, Cuba.
McDonald's and Starbucks,
Can barely contain their
Benevolent enthusiasm
To keep the island
Well fed and caffeinated,
True philanthropists of the world.
Overweight tourists from the south
Will land on the beachhead
in relentless waves.

Michael Oropollo, Jr.

"The Cuban people are very pretty,
I didn't know they could have
Blonde hair and blue eyes."
Another victory for the forces of good,
The sound mind of capitalism
will bring prosperity.
The Cubans freed from their bondage,
will rejoice at the opportunities that await,
like animals at the zoo.

Thoughts

To The Stars We Will Return
X.

teacher- Come 'ere, I'm going teach you a
lesson about life. You're a young man on the
cusp of adulthood and you need to know the
inevitable future of all things human.
(pause)
Teacher- Have you ever looked at a cancer
cell, son.
Student- Excuse me, sir?
Teacher- A cell! A human cell that has been
taken over by a cancer cell!
Student- uh I believe so sir, I took
biology last semester we went over that.
Teacher- Good! Do you know the process of
the cancer disease?
Student- What are you talking abo-
Teacher- Think! Come on now. What do you
pay all that money for if they don't even teach
you how to think, now come on! The process of
cancer! Do you know what it is!
Student- Well, yes sir. A cell has a
defect. And then that cell multiplies creating
more cancer cells and more cancer cells.
The cancer grows and grows, multiplies and
multiplies eventually killing the person it
infects.
Teacher- There it is, kid. That's right.
Student- And this person that was
perfectly healthy before they had cancer,
now becomes sicker and sicker as the cancer
multiplies and spreads.
Teacher- Now have you ever seen a picture
of the earth from outer space.
Student- From outer space?

Michael Oropollo, Jr.

Teacher- Yes! From outer space! Like ehh-- taken from one of those space shuttles?

Student- Well, yea of course.

Teacher- Don't of course me! I know they sure as shit don't teach you for the sake of educating you. I don't know what you have and haven't seen!

Student- I've seen a picture of earth from a space shuttle.

Teacher- ok, ok.

Teacher- what do you see in those pictures of earth?

Student- I'm totally confused..

Teacher- Do you see a perfectly green, healthy earth? Perfectly green land and perfectly blue ocean... as far as your young, impressionable eye can see?

Student- well, yea, kinda.

Student- you can see big cities and stuff. Like you can see Los Angeles, and New York City, Beijing, Mexico City. A bunch of cities, all over the place.

Teacher- You sure can. And they aren't getting smaller are they? They are getting bigger. These dark, grey swathes of human civilization grow and multiply while the green and blue swathes of earth become consumed by them.

Teacher- Now do you know how they treat cancer nowadays.

Student- chemotherapy, surgery, radiation, drugs, uhh I don't kn-

Teacher- Don't tell me you don't because you do know! You just said it.

Teacher- That's right, we use these methods to eradicate cancer from the body.

Thoughts

The infected body will suffer through these treatments, sometimes even causing horrific, permanent side effects, just to eradicate the cancer from their body. Someone who has cancer will take any action, any treatment, regardless of how drastic it is; just to remove the cancer from they're body. They will go to any length to remove this disease that is destroying them from the inside out. Right?

Student- Well, yea, of course they would. They want to be healthy again, cancer-free again.

Teacher- And what happens when that person is cancer free, son?

Student- They are healthy again.

Teacher- Right and?

Student- I don't know. Do whatever they were doing before the cancer showed up.

Teacher- Exactly.

Teacher- Their life goes on.

XI.

One day I'll be reading a book to my son
It'll have animals- rhinos, giraffes, and ti-
gers
He'll get carried off into another world,
his own parallel universe of runaway fantasy,
That only a child can create.
But ill inevitably have to answer questions
Too painful to answer.
I shouldn't have to answer.
While I'm reading my son a book
About rhinos, giraffes and tigers.
I'll have to explain to him what it was like,
When rhinos, giraffes, and tigers roamed the
earth.
Like I'm some sort of prehistoric caveman,
That walked into the wrong time machine,
And is being interrogated by the most curious
of scientists.
"They roamed the plains and the jungles.
Before we built malls and super highways
Over their watering holes and through their
migration patterns."
A key piece of information needed to fill in
the blanks
Of the fantasy world he's creating in his head.
He'll smile, satisfied with this answer.
Blissfully unaware of the
Gravity, and
Heaviness,
Of his question.

XII.

Burst into the new age digital millennium
shotgun blast there is no stopping
or slowing down.
Obsolete are our institutions.
School system, social relations,
Religion, judicial system
Playing checkers in a time of 3-D chess.
Like my old boss,
Still using windows '98.
Still caught up in the quarrels of lines on a
map
Like the Germans,
Like the British,
Like the Romans.
Stare into the sky on a starry night,
The answer so painfully obvious.
And inconveniently ignored,
Like Dad's drinking problem,
And your son's junk habit.
The evolution of man
Means to an end,
We have succeeded, no.
Barely begun.
while I stare into that starry night,
in total silence,
the thought strikes me.
Like a head-on collision with a tree
at 80 mph, drunk on Christmas eve.
If we do not make our next home
Amongst one of those stars,
the matter of our species will return to them.
From The Stars We Are Born

XIII.

of a mountain
broken off
fruit of erosion of a great sea
or a meteor,
or earthquake
pulverized to dust,
rich,
fertile
dust.
he grew.
and blossomed,
how many times?
Too many to count.
Centuries,
Millennia,
Of pulverization,
Dust,
Rich and fertile,
Growing and blossoming.
Megalodon, king of the sea
a hummingbird,
dog,
maybe my old bull mastiff
A human being.
Someday a man on Mars.
Life experiencing itself,
Over and over and over,
Pulverized to dust again,
And now we cry?
Not
The maggots
And worms.
Or the birds,
Or squirrels,

Thoughts

The coyotes will surely
Give thanks to him.
He will not cry either,
Just change
And grow.
Spirit becomes one
With the whole,
Back to the infinite.
To visit our dreams,
And overwhelm us
With emotions,
When necessary.
A wink and nudge
Somewhere from the divine.
Like a thought.
Can't be proven
But it surely is there.
The scientist puts down his paper
and pounds the table.
Demanding proof.
"Everything,
In the whole,
In the infinite,
Must be quantifiable!"
He reads his paper,
And comments
On his horoscope.
Favorable.
But I feel
It.
How can I measure that?
Is there a tape measure long enough?
To wrap around the infinite.
Of course.
Infinite tape measure.
The scientist was right.

Michael Oropollo, Jr.

Where do the numbers end on this?
and the spirits run amok,
giggling, and dancing,
jumping up and down,
in and out
living in our dreams,
and memories.
And now we have made a joyful mess
Of the infinite.
Wrapped
in infinite tape measure,
The scientist finally pleased.
We've included measurements
just as unsure as him,
but
upset because his horoscope
was off that day.

XIV.

What if all the planets in our solar system,
all the solar systems in our galaxies were
just sprinkles on a cupcake.
Sprinkles on a cupcake?
Yeah sprinkles on a cupcake, right.
See, you got all these sprinkles, they are all
the galaxies we live in,
The frosting we sit on is the dark matter of
the universe.
What about black holes?
Black holes?
Yea what about black holes?
Donuts! Sprinkles on a frosted donut.
Sometimes a sprinkle slides off through the
donut hole,
And there you have it, black holes.
Some universes are intelligent universes,
Similar to the one we live in.
You have intelligent beings
 (I suppose you could call us that,
after all this poem is about sprinkles.),
different species of organisms,
Evolution, technology and the like.
So we are like the cupcakes at a fancy wedding
of some sort
Or at a red carpet after party,
We are some very expensive, well-done cup-
cakes.
Other universes are in constant conflict
Cataclysmic events occur simultaneously
Like our solar system during the Big Bang
Sprinkles flying all over the place
Frosting dark matter spread with no mercy,

Michael Oropollo, Jr.

A dangerous violent universe.
What kind of universe is that?
That's like the cupcakes at a child's party
Toddlers are the gods of that universe,
It's a difficult existence.
So what if we are all sprinkles on a cupcake,
or donut
What's the point, who cares, you're crazy.
If we are just bloody sprinkles on a cupcake,
Why are we taking this thing so damn serious?

The Child's Journey

XV.

Effortlessly suspended,
In the embryonic fluid
Of mother earth,
The universe
Produced.
Produces
A perfect unflawed star
Something's divine design
Continuous,
Complete,
Satisfied.
The fissures split the matrix up
Dividing factions.
The human element
Unnatural to the order
Adam eats the apple,
a child is born.
A vacuum of life before
Adam eats the apple,
A billion times over.
Energy of the physical,
cyclones
the eye of the storm
which seeks more to grow darkness,
War, poverty, hate.
Success, failure.

Michael Oropollo, Jr.

A child is born.

XVI.

my mom dragged me
by my little hand,
as mothers tend to do
through the walls of marble
and coffer ceilings.
Passing portraits of men in suits.
"Mommy who's that?"
"A great man,
CEO of a large enterprise."
"Mommy who's that?"
"A banker...
"an ex president...
the pope..."
"Great Men."
and I jumped
on the tile floor,
from black tile,
to black tile,
because the white ones
were lava.
And we passed
A man,
mopping floors.
"Mommy who's that?"
"Nobody"

Thoughts

XVII.

A child with a heart still open
Picks four leaf clovers
In the meadow
From which he grew.
the source is pure,
as it always is.
cut and stepped on,
The further along the way it goes.
it passes through more hands.
Thrown into the machine,
Ground up by the gears,
Additives cut the purity,
Apparently for the greater good.
Potent and pure truths,
for the maintenance of
a well functioning machine.
The truth is iron clad,
And will tear through gears
Like bullet through flesh.
The final product,
Is heavily diluted.
Containing a small percentage
Of the source,
But overall,
Unrecognizable from it.
the four leaf clover
doesn't exist anyway.
just a powerful alternate reality to
a boy,
and an elusive mirage
to man.

Michael Oropollo, Jr.

XVIII.

what a shame, what a shame
wagging little finger
the old lady
of the neighborhood,
says "I told ya so".
She was right,
She could tell us so
Cause she had seen,
was told before.
Flower children of the free state,
Cast away the chains
That bondage their brains.
Although briefly,
Goddamn did they succeed.
But the road broke their
will, as the road can do.
The ones still left,
Mind went away on a trip
Never to come back.
Once that trip is taken,
And goddamn it was took,
Enlightenment, awakening,
Can't be taken away.
The door had been opened
And although the road can
Shut it, as the road can do,
We know the door is there.
Inviting the next collection
Of travellers to open it up
And cast away the chains.
However temporary it may last.
The ones who maintain the way of things,
will suck resources dry

Thoughts

paving a pretty new road
to break the next travelers' will.
Because the road isn't meant
To be taken on trips,
To have new experiences,
To free us from bondage.
The roads are meant,
To drive to and from work.

Michael Oropollo, Jr.

XIX.

10,000 years of intergalactic war ravaged the
solar system.
A war against holograms that
We couldn't see, or give a concrete definition
of,
But our leader, lover of peace told us they
were there.
And they were coming!
So began the 10,000-year war.
The college I went to
Turned out to be a front,
Harvesting human brains,
And pumping in hot air,
They made a killing off tuition.
And all the elders
Who had been working
In the forced labor camps
Told us we were lazy.
 How useless, and unfulfilling our lives were,
"Your gonna end up in the gutter kid!"
So I thought I'd check out
What the gutter was like.
I crawled through the gutter
And arrived on the other side
To the beautiful meadow,
Hills rolled in every direction,
Vibrant green grass.
Not every gutter led to this meadow,
But only gutters lead here.
We were told places like this couldn't exist,
How long we lived like horses with blinders
on,
Here I am. First human I know to see the other
side of things.

Thoughts

Bondage

XX.

The illusion
of a full soul
and no one to give it to.
The last day of summer
before high school.
Sunday night,
before the test,
and I still haven't studied.
A bad neighborhood,
hostile territory,
the enemy surrounds
on all sides,
with nowhere to retreat.
Colors turn to black and white
and grey.
So much grey.
The beast starts to talk,
Reality becomes skewed,
Perception becomes
limited, like a horse
With blinders on,
Racing down a track.
Inability to connect
with other people,
the sound
of my own thoughts
Is quite deafening.
Now I've spun the wheel
a game of Russian roulette,
I have no control,
over where
or when
it will stop.

Michael Oropollo, Jr.

I try as hard as I can
to get the gears in motion,
but they just wont go.
Big, shiny, new gears.
Doused in mud, wont even spin.
A stuck eyesore.
Producing nothing of value.
Catatonic state of permanent limbo,
My eyes a transparent sheet of glass,
The windows to the soul, no ones home.
Stare at the blank sheet of paper in front of
me.
I wish the words could just write themselves
The story just right itself,
But I know writing doesn't work like that.
I should just pack up my things,
Hit the highway,
And chase the sun east until it hits the ocean.
Button up for the cold winter ahead.
The pieces don't fit, they can't fit.
This state obsolete and permanent.
Drew a 3 & 7, not a hand worth playing.
Better fold this one before I get caught in my
own bluff.
Best I just close my eyes and wait
For a new hand to be dealt.
No use getting shot,
Trying to cheat a lousy hand.
The game starts over
The change is always permanent.

XXI.

Old times with a new friend.
I learn more about myself.
Holding a mirror up
With a flashlight.
See myself. Illuminated, shadowed.
What's left to the subconscious,
Boiled to the surface.
Gentle, soft affect
Contrasts the chaos within.
Tranquility reflects
The internal monologue.
Machine gun firing
at Enemy ghosts in the dark.
Mirage of the ego caught
Like a pest
In a game trap.

Michael Oropollo, Jr.

XXII.

Traffic buzzing, midtown new york city 9 am,
Traffic, rushing, los angeles 405 9 am,
a hustle here, a dollar there,
Clients need me, markets need me
no time to spare
Wait in line. Wait in line. Wait in line.
Catch a glimpse of the TV behind the counter,
Markets up.
coffee, bagel, $10.99? fuck it keep the cha-
The market! Up! 600 points overnight! Up! Up !
Up!
Dash to the office I fret and fret
Buy low sell high,
All that bullshit.
Drinks after work, I can buy the house.
But ill just sip this old fashion and
puff my blouse.
Back home to the wife and kids I drudge,
Sound and fast asleep my wife I nudge,
Dreaming of her high school sweetheart,
She doesn't budge.
My life of success I'll never change my course,
When I die spread my ashes on the golf course.

XXIII.

Bought a new Porsche, just to crash it.
A mansion in the hills to hide bodies in the
attic.
My smile is for the camera, my soul in panic.
I'm a puppet used to feed everyone's habit.
My life is the viper and I am the rabbit.
I am like you and you like me,
When the piper calls you gotta pay the fee.
Like leeches and crickets in the dead king's
tomb,
I am no longer mine, I am yours to consume.

XXIV.

I don't balk at those who worship
at the altar of god,
However vain and insincere some may be.
But the killing and holy wars,
terrorism, and hatred.
The money and conspiracy and lies
yeah, yeah, yeah, we know.
The starlit altar, in churches that used to be
holy,
Marquee that once held names of the divine.
Just another altar raped and pillaged.
By those corrupted.
I once was a man of faith
Had my idols hung on my wall.
Idols now dead and gone,
the torch passed fewer and farther between.
Too many replaced, not for the
divine work that they do,
but for their ability to please those who
blindly pray.
A lack of natural selection,
Idols shoved down our throats
By the money making machine.
And while the Christians
And Muslims
And Jews are mocked
by
The masses
are
devoutly worshipping the
ghost written and lip synced.

Thoughts

XXV.

Shot
out of Orion's bow
The spear tip of his arrow
At the speed of light
Roaring
Its way through space.
Burning
Hot and bright
A glowing red ember in the sky.
Tearing
Its way through dark matter.
It fades,
and
sputters,
To the end of its run,
Burnt out
like a jaded rock star.

XXVI.

The Admiral had plans
For all he could be.
Matador of powers greater than he,
Dethroned like the others
By a storm of the sea.
The Emperor reflected
On his power and might,
Immortal and invincible
They slit his throat in the night.
Many kings lie in shallow graves
Admirals die in the oceans waves,
Even Jesus was buried inside of a cave.
No giant of man will ever be saved
No road to salvation is ever be paved.

Thoughts

Evolution

XXVII.

I am pleased to say I have witnessed,
The most advanced phase of human evolution,
We have ever reached.
Five fingers have been replaced,
by just an index finger and thumb.
All that is necessary to use our smartphones,
thus enabling us to be more social.
The brain is no longer overworked,
by having to pick up on social cues.
Vocal chords no longer strained,
by verbal communication.
And ears no longer burdened with listening,
All communication done via text message.
Children no longer have to climb trees,
or skateboard down steep hills.
Adults no longer have to race cars
at high speeds, or climb the world's
largest, most dangerous mountains.
We have eliminated danger.
The human race can now live safely,
In the comfort of our home 24/7
Thanks to virtual reality.
Jobs are no longer needed,
In this advanced society of ours.
Robots now do all the work,
and have freed us to be more productive
with our time on earth.
I am pleased to live
In this exciting phase
of human history.
They say pretty soon,
we will be able to live in total virtual reali-
ty.

Michael Oropollo, Jr.

Not even needing to go through the inconve-
nience of
Living life ourselves.

XXVIII.

Castle walls built on golden shores.
Shoulders of giants on top we stand
Never seeing above the tree-line.
A kaleidoscope of stained glass windows,
church steeples that reach for the sun,
cast the darkest shadow of the deepest black.
The land of riches,
And spoils of war.
Excess easily accessed.
The land of corpses and ghosts
Bodies with no souls, souls with no bodies.
The disease of more.
I wanted and I wanted,
I got and got,
It could never fill the hole.
Shoveled in more stuff,
and more stuff.
Coal into the furnace,
could never keep it burning hot enough.
Burnt out, scorched earth
Lifestyle of the damned,
Always asking why, when, and how.
No surprise to me,
How we feel so alone,
With 350 million around.

XXIX.

Shelves of dapper dressed gentlemen
And their blonde counterparts.
Replaced with acid soaked
Shells of impulses and bad manners.
Wanna be wiseguys,
Reality star wheelmen for the mob from back
east.
High school sweethearts of the Midwest,
Paralyzed with fear,
Hold onto each others arms,
Wearing masks of smiles,
Cause at this point   fuck it.
Musicians, actors, personalities,
Famous in a world other than this
Try their best to look the part,
Never buying the knockoff brands
And spending way beyond their means.
Everyone keeping up appearances
In a city of plastic.
Terrified of this moment,
Of every moment,
Fear of a connection,
Connection with another human being,
The thought alone is paralyzing.
Head deep in phones,
Bumping into one another,
Chickens with their heads cut off.
Rushing where?
They don't even know.
But. must be rushing,
If plastic isn't constantly moving,
It melts under the lights.
What if I don't look like I'm rushing?
What if I look content with where I am?

Thoughts

What if I am in no hurry at all?
Social suicide.
The store buzzes with noise,
None of which conversational.
Everyone's learned social anxiety disorder,
Pavlov's dogs on a bad acid trip.

Michael Oropollo, Jr.

Purgatory

XXX.

Mad scientists create their solutions
Dark and raw and potent as hell.
Like a bottle of Everclear
or opium straight off the poppy.
Somewhere from production to consumption,
it gets watered down,
and cut,
to make it more fit for sale,
more palatable to the general public.
Mainstream.
And they censor your art.
And they turn your punk rock,
into corporate mall pop,
recycle the same old movie ideas
with sequels worse than the last.
They create a million Tyler Durdens
"And we are very, very pissed off..."
til one day the levee breaks and
rushes forth in the water of the minds
held back in contempt.

XXXI.

You were absent when they were giving in-
structions.
Missed the rule book on how to navigate this.
Boundaries created on a plane no boundaries
exist
They make the rules as they go, the boundaries
get smaller,
confine you to where you're needed the least.
We all enter this collection of space and time,
this perfect, unlikely, improbable universe,
perfect beings, of light and spirit.
Ideas waiting to be unleashed,
to create and love
to foster and teach.
We are numbed.
The social opiate.
Pacifies and soothes.
Forgetting our responsibility to the cosmos.
Exist and consume, and live to be consumed,
fate predetermined a life Galileo.
Suck the light from the stars,
Don't try to fit in.

XXXII.

Alarm set 7:30 sharp,
9 p.m. past my bed time,
I lay down to do some writing.
Some wild tale, reckless and careless,
reminds me of my true self,
before I choose to lie under
a loosely stitched blanket
of responsibilities.
I thought looked good to others,
hesitantly inspired, I write.
Madly. Feverishly.
Like a starved man
who was stranded on a boat
for weeks.
Just rescued to shore.
Pound the keys with
raw passion and aggression,
how I used to play sports
when I was younger.
My default mode.
My true self.
Unknowingly slip through time.
Time is relative,
Time flies when you're having fun.
Einstein's theory,
Something like that,
Doesn't matter.
It's all fair game,
no mercy, no one to offend,
nothing to lose,
total freedom.
I slip through time,
covered in sweat over my keyboard,
my alarm keeps ringing.

XXXIII.

This will not change your life,
It doesn't mean anything.
Continue reading if you
have nothing better to do.
Of course you don't.
I didn't study English,
at some fancy liberal arts school
I have no trust fund or
Connections with some queer
holier than thou conspiracy of trendsetters.
I won't further your socialist agenda,
and you are offended easily
as you seem to get.
So much so, you walk out of
your SoHo coffee shop,
disgusted.
Your originality, unoriginal;
so similar in your difference.
Little cliques
made up of those
too cool for cliques.
I told you this poem was meaningless
I won't make a dollar off of it
I think I'll print it and burn it
Just for a
Laugh
at the lack of freedom,
locked in new cages just like the old cages
but cooler.

Michael Oropollo, Jr.

The Man's Journey

XXXIV.

I have yet to find an experience that provides
me
and connects me - To the source,
like floating in the ocean.
I can close my eyes and float,
like we float in the womb
long before we learn expectations, temptations
and all of the acquired insanity.
As soon as my toes touch the cool Pacific,
on a brisk, chill morning,
a metamorphosis occurs.
Transference from the singular to the whole,
no longer myself, no longer an isolated vessel
navigating space.
I become part of the space between.
The infinite and whole.
When I float out there,
the morning sun shining through the marine
layer
hits the water a certain way
its texture looks like a million pieces of
thread
laid side by side.
The most perfect painting of light, color, and
texture
I think to myself:
In this moment I am as close as I will ever be.

XXXV.

Sunny
skies,
clear weather,
haven't seen
a cloud for quite
awhile now.
cool ocean
breeze, it's all
very. pleasant.
days,
weeks,
months on end.
Every so often,
a desire burns
so hot,
white heat,
in my core.
for a rainstorm.
A violent,
chaotic
rainstorm.
Winds screaming,
howling
blowing,
it's raining sideways.
Thunder
a thousand bombs,
lightning,
an artillery strike
from the sky.
Yes.
Sometimes.
While I relax on my beach,
my little slice of paradise,

Michael Oropollo, Jr.

with the ocean breeze blowing through,
and the sun beating down,
on my sun kissed face,
I crave
a most
violent storm.
Sometimes,
for pure
novelty.
Sometimes
out of the spite
of others.
Sometimes,
just to wash
all of this away.

XXXVI.

A long, fulfilling life I had led,
success after success.
I had built enterprises,
empires, a titan of industry,
decided the fate of men
through the stroke of a pen.
I had won the rat race,
And so I became weary.
Worn down and jaded with the world.
Seeking new life, I went back to where
it all began for us.
Took to the open ocean,
via a tested and true companion,
Lady Liberty.
When I left Newport, Rhode Island
I was looking for something.
Whether I knew it or not.
Drawn to the ocean
like settlers drawn west,
chasing ideas and tales.
I had made been traveling 77 days.
Around the Cape of Good Hope,
through the Mediterranean.
And as I was traveling through the deep, un-
mapped Pacific,
I didn't know it at the time, but lady liberty
was living up to her name.
A violent storm shipwrecked her,
exactly where she was leading me,
as I look back, I realize I never was captain-
ing that ship.
A deserted island is where I pen this, under a
coconut tree.
A few weeks after lady liberty fulfilled her

Michael Oropollo, Jr.

cosmic responsibility.
Fruitful and abundant,
and isolated.
A plane has flown over,
I think I spotted a ship in the distance,
I can't be sure.
While I didn't know
what I was looking for when I left,
the answer has revealed itself now.
I will put this letter in a bottle.
Throw it as far as I can into the ocean,
just for a laugh.
And after a few more weeks,
maybe I'll make a signal fire,
flag down one of those planes
that occasionally fly overhead.

Thoughts

XXXVII.

A string knit hammock strewn between two palm
trees,
is where I'll park myself for the day.
And I'll sway with the wind,
with a shit eating grin on my face.
Like a fat little pig rolling around in the
mud.
There's nothing to worry about.
Fret over.
No nerves worth pinching.
Hair worth pulling out.
None of it matters.
What I sell.
How much I sell it for,
Who I sell it to.
Nope. Doesn't matter.
The perfect matrix of time and space,
of fate and destiny,
of love and unity
is not concerned with any of it.
So today, I'll just lay in this hammock
And sway.
Back
And forth and
back and
forth and back
and...

XXXVIII.

She came to me in a dream,
and I walked out of a large
skyscraper that was reaching
towards boundless sky.
The crowd was huge,
buzzing about.
People jumping,
And laughing,
she was holding a sign.
J.B.L.
I walked right by her.
she cried and cried.
No sooner I took a step away,
I took a step back.
Agitated and in a hurry,
I asked her what's wrong.
Her friend answered
"she's been following you for months,
traveling hundreds of miles,
to be where you are."
With a face full of tears,
and a small smile,
she nodded.
I woke up,
from that dream,
and tried my hardest,
to fall back asleep,
to go back to that moment,
grabbing onto a fist full of sand.

XXXIX.

I wake up, don't know how I got here.
An alien from another dimension.
Dropped off at the wrong planet by the mother
ship
the mother ship doesn't make mistakes.
I creeped and clawed, hemmed and hawed.
Navigating this alien planet and its native
species,
learning as I go.
Failed experiment after failed experiment.
Trial by fire,
Mother nature has no mercy
The native species has no mercy
A chameleon, one of the best in this solar sys-
tem I am.
A steep learning curve, but once this chame-
leon learns
how to change colors
I can make the aurora borealis jealous.
Lesson one: the mother makes no mistakes.
Lesson two: the mother doesn't owe you any-
thing.
The learning curve is a steep one,
But I find my groove,
The rhythm of this dimension.
All dimensions have their own rhythm.
Although this native species
exerts maximum control over this one,
leads it like an elephant in the circus.
Or so they think. Try as they might and try
they do.
Foreign leader of this native species,
Supreme chameleon,
Manchurian candidate,

Michael Oropollo, Jr.

The immigrant who learned
the rules of the game
And won.

Thoughts

Freedom

XL.

full body visceral inhalation.
and exhale.
Expanding and contracting.
this moment,
moments that came before.
Experiences in   a   jigsaw puzzle.
The image becomes clearer piece by piece,
after long hours sitting at the coffee table.
Loves,
great loves,
gained and lost.
Loved ones as well.
Life and death,
seething anger, disease.
Moments beautifully divine,
and macabrely dark.
The action shots of the image
in the puzzle.
The mundane details not to be ignored either.
The background, the borders.
hours of waiting in lines,
traffic, frustrations, menial work.
All necessary;
so the totality,
and true essence of the image
on the puzzle
Can be completed.
A full and complete life.
Inhale, exhale
Expand, contract.
Rain bouncing off my forehead,
Northwestern chill in my spine,
Misty morning fog settled in.

Michael Oropollo, Jr.

All of it absorbed into my being,
As I expand
Infinitely,
Splitting and multiplying
Billions of times per second
Cells continuously dividing,
The universe exponentially expanding,
Piece after piece of the puzzle
Rapidly locking together one after another,
The image I'll never be able
To see what it is when it's finished,
But in this moment it is clearer
Than anything I've ever known.
Release.
Relief.
I don't even want to
Touch it.
Or attempt
To control it.
I could only ruin it.
It is so satisfying,
Overwhelming positively
To sit
in the cradle of the soul
to let it be and to be.
To finish a puzzle
I will never see completed.

The State Of Current Affairs: Part 2
XLI.

Contemporary monopoly
on creativity
of symmetry,
simple similes,
artistic expression assimilates
pathetically .
Gatekeepers of modern pop culture,
three blind mice,
with third eye's blind
peddle garbage
infiltrate the adolescent mind.
Corrupted culture vultures,
Pick what's left off the bones,
Leave the rest to rot
In the desert heat.
Close the blinds of their homes,
secure in their false dome
while their country withers.
The final years of empire Rome.
Information at our fingertips,
The show has dumbed down the script,
No need to burn books anymore.
Media control, loose lips sink ships.
Maybe you'll see me walking down the street,
whistling a tune, in the middle of June,
When revolution
drives the king out of town.
They'll catch him right at the border, Put this
all back in order,
And right before they gun him down,
They whisper in his ear while a smile and a
jeer,
Heavy lies the crown.

www.ingramcontent.com/pod-product-compliance
Lightning Source LLC
Chambersburg PA
CBHW050428110726
47899CB00008B/2895